DIY for
Your Dog

DIY for
Your Dog
Toys, Treats, and Treasures to Make

Rachelle Blondel

STC Craft | New York

contents

play

wear

introduction

From the moment their little wet noses arrive on the doorstep, a dog becomes part and parcel of the everyday goings on in your household. Always there to welcome you home with an eager wagging tail and eyes just sparkling with love, to perch on your lap when you are feeling a little less than perfect, a dog's heart has no limits and will love you for every second of every day, even if you are upset with them for chewing the back door frame. So why not whip up a whole host of crafty odds and ends to show your dog how cherished he or she is?

As you flip through the pages of this book, all sorts of crafty projects to crochet, knit, sew, and bake will catch your eye. Each and every one offers a lovely, but practical, item to show your pooch that they are loved and cared for in every way. Plus, they enable you to personalize your doggy paraphernalia to match your own decorating style rather than having to settle for the everyday mundane doggy stuff, which too often comes in various shades of brown.

Make them a warm cozy bed to snuggle into during those long hours of sleep, topped with a knitted blanket for burrowing into. When the days turn wet and nippy, keep them warm on your daily walk with a made-to-measure dog coat. And when those sunny days show their smiles, dress them up in a jaunty neckerchief or dapper bow tie for their saunter around the neighborhood.

We are all thoughtful of where our food comes from nowadays and what it is made from. If you whip up a few dog treats using ingredients from your kitchen cupboard, you will know exactly what your dog is munching on and that it is keeping them healthy and bright.

Everything you make for your dog not only gives you the joy of crafting your day away, but it also shows them how special they are as proud owners of an array of handmade goodness which in turn will be chewed, rummaged in, chased about, and proudly worn, all with a wagging tail and a thankful heart.

It seems fitting at this point to say a huge thank you to all the dogs that have wandered my path with me. Each and every one of you has brought a little bit of sunshine.

eat

This chapter is full of tasty, wholesome, and easy-to-make treats. Whip up a batch or two, so you know exactly what is going in your dog's tummy. These treats are ideal to use for training, a munch to say I love you, and even a birthday cake to celebrate your pooch's special day.

Everyone loves a cake on their birthday, so why not indulge your dog with a little treat on theirs? Banana and honey cakes (baked individually so your pooch doesn't over-do it) are a delectable treat when topped with a delicious cream cheese and peanut butter frosting. Go to town with sprinkles and carob chips to make your dog's day extra special.

doggie birthday cake

2 bananas

2 tablespoons canola oil

I egg, lightly beaten

3 tablespoons (45ml) natural yogurt

I tablespoon honey

1¾ cups (200g) whole-wheat flour

I teaspoon baking soda

TOPPING FOR I CAKE

I tablespoon cream cheese

I tablespoon peanut butter

carob chips*, optional

sprinkles, optional

mini dog treats, optional

MAKES 6
MUFFIN-SIZE
CAKES

1 Preheat the oven to 350°F (180°C).

2 Mash the bananas and mix with the oil, egg, yogurt, and honey in a large bowl until everything is well combined.

3 Stir in the flour and baking soda, then spoon the batter into a 6-cup muffin tin and bake for 15 minutes. Allow to cool.

4 Beat the cream cheese and peanut butter together and then swirl, pipe, or spoon the frosting onto the top of the muffin.

5 Adorn with carob chips, sprinkles, and a mini dog treat or two and wish your doggie a very merry birthday.

Remaining cakes can be frozen without frosting for up to 3 months.

*Please do not use normal chocolate as it can be extremely harmful to your dog.

A birthday is not indeed a birthday without cake... even for dogs

We all need a cool-down treat during the hot days of summer and the same is true of our four-legged friends: with their furry coats they find it hard to keep cool on days when the temperature soars. These yummy frozen snacks will keep your hound chilled and entertained for a while and are quick and easy to prepare.

doggie pops

I banana, sliced

I apple, cored and chopped

5–6 strawberries

a handful of mint leaves

I cup (200ml) natural yogurt

a spoonful of flax seed oil, optional

mini bones or chew sticks, optional

MAKES ABOUT 24

1 Place the fruit, mint, yogurt, and flax seed oil, if using, in a blender and blitz until creamy and smooth.

2 Pour the puree into silicon mini-muffin tins, or any other suitable container—small yogurt containers placed on a tray work well—and place upright in the freezer.

3 After about 30 minutes, check to see if they are starting to become firm and then (if using) pop a bone or chew stick in each one. If the pops aren't frozen enough to support the bones, leave them to freeze for a while longer.

4 Freeze overnight, then remove the pops from the containers and transfer to a freezer bag for easier storage.

All dogs love treats, especially ones they can chew. Sweet potatoes are a great source of dietary fiber for your dog, along with vitamin B$_6$, vitamin C, beta carotene, and manganese. These chewy strips are simple to make and will soon become a firm favorite.

sweet potato chew strips

YOU WILL NEED

I large sweet potato

MAKES 12–15

1 Turn your oven onto the lowest setting.

2 Slice the potato into thin strips and spread over a baking tray lined with parchment paper. Bake for 30 minutes. Turn the strips over, then bake for another 30 minutes.

3 If, after this, there are still any soft areas, turn and bake again until they are firm.

4 Allow the strips to cool completely before storing in an airtight container for up to one week.

Bake some wholesome goodness for your pooch by making these homemade dog biscuits. Made with carrots, coconut, and peanut butter, they will be loved by your dog and you can be assured he or she is getting a healthy, natural treat, too.

dog biscuits

YOU WILL NEED

3 carrots, peeled and roughly chopped

1⅔ cups (150g) oatmeal

1 tablespoon coconut oil

1 tablespoon peanut butter

2 eggs

a spoonful chia or flax seeds, optional

MAKES 15–20

1 Preheat the oven to 350°F (180°C) and line a large baking sheet with parchment paper.

2 Place the carrots and oatmeal in a food processer and blend until both are finely chopped.

3 Add the coconut oil, peanut butter, and eggs and blend again, then empty the mixture into a bowl and chill for 30 minutes.

4 Place teaspoons of the mixture onto the prepared baking sheet and carefully flatten with a spoon. Bake for 20 minutes.

5 Transfer to a rack to cool. Store biscuits in an airtight container for up to 1 week.

doggie treats tin

Just to make sure there is no doubt who those delicious looking homemade treats belong to, store them in their very own treat tin so there is no confusion when snacking late at night. Reuse dog food cans to make these useful little storage containers that will look good sitting on the Handy Wall Shelf (see page 42), which you must make to keep everything dog-related neat and tidy.

YOU WILL NEED

food cans in various sizes
fine sandpaper
spray paint
strong glue
plastic toy dogs
food cover lids
brown kraft paper, rubber stamps, and ink pad

1 Begin by thoroughly cleaning the food tins, paying extra attention to the inside.

2 Rub down any sharp edges on the inside of the can with sandpaper.

3 Place the cans on a covered surface, preferably outside, and spray the outside of the cans with at least two coats of paint (follow the manufacturer's specific instructions). Leave the tins to dry for at least 24 hours, or longer, if possible.

4 Glue the toy dogs to the lids. Allow the glue to set and completely cure before using (follow the manufacturer's guidelines for curing times).

5 Using a strip of brown paper as a label, write or stamp the contents or some other catchy title on the paper so that you can remember what's inside each tin. Fill with various doggie treats and items.

If you're always in search of the perfect dog bowl (one that doesn't spill its contents as dinner is gobbled up), then give this one a try. Using heavy-bottomed cereal bowls will ensure dinnertime is a far more civilized affair, with no chance of a broken bowl after a munching frenzy. The fact that they can often be picked up for next to nothing at thrift shops and are nearly unbreakable makes them a great choice for a food vessel. Adding a nifty blackboard square means you can chalk in your dog's name to make the bowl their very own.

this is my bowl

a sturdy or heavy-bottomed cereal bowl (the size depends on the size of your dog)

masking tape

plastic wrap

blackboard paint or spray paint

craft knife

chalk

1 Give your bowl a really good soapy scrub with a scouring pad to remove any surface dirt.

2 Mask off a border around the shape you wish to paint, and cover the rest of the bowl in plastic wrap, taping down the edges.

3 Paint the unmasked area on your bowl with several thin coats of paint (follow the manufacturer's specific instructions). Leave to dry.

4 Remove all the tape and plastic wrap and tidy up any wayward paint edges with a sharp craft knife.

5 Scribble your pet's name in chalk on the blackboard label and wait for dinnertime.

nest

Make your dog as comfy as possible as he or she whiles away the hours in the land of nod, snoring peacefully, snuggled up with a handmade bone pillow, a knitted blanket, or in a rather fancy bed.

Make a special place for your dog to sleep by reusing an old drawer, suitcase, "seen better days" basket, or wine crate. By adding a lovely lining and popping in a comfy pillow, your dog's bed won't look out of place in whatever room they choose to rest their weary head. Everything is removable and washable, so there will be no chance of nasty odors or unwelcome bugs.

a bed to sleep in

1 Before you begin sewing, clean the base of your bed and make it safe and free from any loose pieces, sharp nails, hinges, or anything else that could harm your dog.

2 Measure the base length and width, then add a ½-inch (1cm) seam allowance to each side. Cut a piece of fabric in this size.

3 Measure the length and width of each box side and add a 2-inch (5cm) seam allowance to the top edge and a ½-inch (1cm) seam allowance to all other edges. Cut 4 pieces of fabric to these sizes.

4 Stitch the sides to the base (see below), leaving ½ inch (1cm) unstitched at each end of the seams.

5 Pin the corner seams together and stitch to create a box-shaped lining.

6 Neaten the top edge with an overlock, serging, or zigzag stitch, and then press over 2 inches (5cm) of fabric to the wrong side.

7 Overlap one end of the elastic onto the other end and pin. Check to see if the loop fits around the top of the bed, making adjustments if necessary, then sew the ends together to make a flat join.

8 Stretch and pin the elastic evenly around the top edge of the wrong side of the lining, and then, using the stretch-stitch setting on your sewing machine, stitch with a wide zigzag, pulling the elastic taut as you sew.

9 Place the liner into the bed, folding the elastic edge over the top to keep it secure.

10 Pop in a comfy cushion (make one to size, see page 34) and place in a sunny spot.

All dogs like to snuggle down into a warm cozy blanket and dream of chasing rabbits. So why not knit them this super soft, fancy-looking blanket to add to their bed? Maybe then the plump pile of sofa cushions will no longer call their name!

knitted dog blanket

YOU WILL NEED

17½ ounces (500g) worsted or bulky wool in colors of your choice

1¾ ounces (50g) worsted wool for edging

K/10½ circular needle

J/10 crochet hook

Note: Each stripe of color on the blanket will use 3½ ounces (100g) of yarn.

Blanket

1 Cast on 129 stitches.

2 Knit in garter stitch (knit every row) for 40 rows.

3 Change color and knit in garter stitch for 40 rows.

4 Repeat steps 2–3 until you have 5 alternating blocks of colors. Cast off and sew in the ends.

Edging

1 Join the worsted yarn into the first stitch on the right side of the blanket, on the bottom short edge.

2 Chain 1 and then single crochet into each stitch to the end. Turn and repeat for five rows.

3 Chain 1, *work a single crochet into each of the next two stitches, slip stitch, chain 3, slip stitch into next stitch to form a picot. Repeat from * to end.

4 Repeat edging steps 1–3 once on the top edge. Bind off and sew in the ends.

Dogs love blankets nearly as much as they love bones

Give your dog a warm, snuggly place to sprawl out and sink into with this comfy bed. The thermal-quilt effect gives extra warmth, which will encourage more slumber time and a provide safe space for your dog to chill out and relax.

rest-a-weary-head bed

a piece of fusible web interfacing (such as Wonder Under) to fit chosen design

a small piece of contrasting fabric for appliqué

2 pieces 19 × 26-inch (47 × 67cm) fabric, for cover

a single duvet folded into quarters, edges hand stitched together to form a pillow, or a ready-made pillow form

1 Trace either the bone or paw template on pages 41 and 52 onto the paper side of your interfacing. Following the manufacturer's instructions, iron onto the wrong side of your piece of contrasting fabric.

2 Carefully cut out the design and place it on the right side of one of your pieces of cover fabric. When you are happy with the placement, iron it onto the fabric.

3 Using a narrow zigzag stitch, machine-sew around the edges of your design.

4 Lay the second piece of cover fabric onto the first, right sides together, and pin or tack around the edges. Leave an opening at one end to enable you to insert the pillow. You could add a zipper or envelope opening at this stage if you wish.

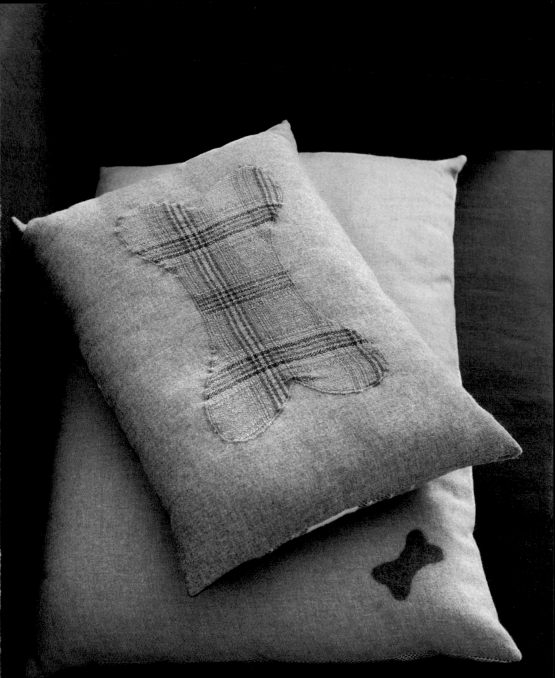

5 Leaving a ½-inch (1cm) seam, start sewing at one end of the opening and stitch around the edge until you reach the other end of the opening. Turn your cover over and repeat the above step following the previous seam line. This will give your cushion seams extra strength.

6 Clip the corners and then finish the seam with an overlock or narrow zigzag stitch, to prevent the edges from fraying when the pillow is washed.

7 Turn your cover to the right side and ease out the corners. Carefully steam the entire cover to shape.

8 Insert your duvet cushion, lining up the corners and making sure it is laying flat inside, then hand stitch the opening closed. Place in a draft-free corner and watch your dog nap the day away.

The pillow and cover are designed to be washed together, but if you would prefer to wash them separately, add a zipper or make a simple envelope cover which can be removed from the pillow.

Make a smaller pillow by folding the duvet in half again and adjust your measurements accordingly.

If there is a pillow and a dog together in the same space, then no matter how small the pillow, you will always find the dog balancing on it trying to catch a few winks of sleep. So why not treat your dog to a pillow or two of their very own in this fun bone shape? Then there can be no doubt about whose pillow belongs to whom!

bone pillow

YOU WILL NEED

2 pieces of fabric large enough to fit the template

polyester cushion filling

1 Enlarge the bone template on page 41 on a copy machine to the size that you require for your pillow (remember to allow for a ½-inch [1cm] seam allowance).

2 Cut out two bone shapes from your fabric and pin them together with the right sides facing.

3 Stitch around the edge of the bone, leaving the seam open where indicated on the template.

4 Trim the seam allowance and snip the seams on all the curves.

5 Turn the pillow right side out and stuff with the polyester filling.

6 Sew the opening closed.

Best seat in the house!

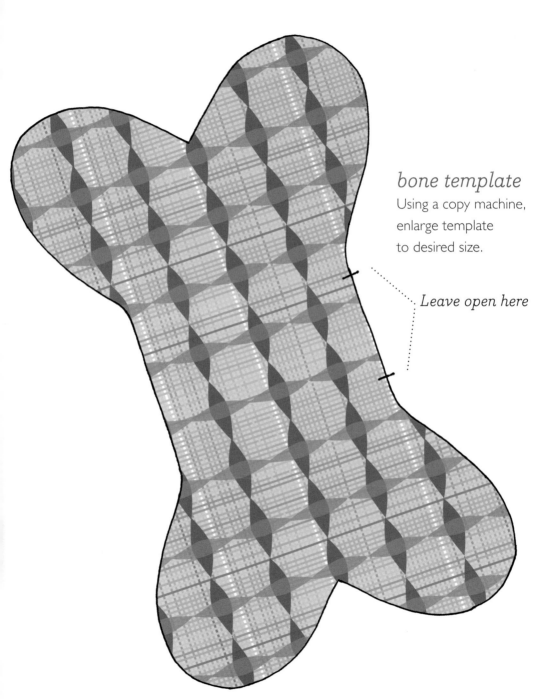

bone template
Using a copy machine,
enlarge template
to desired size.

Leave open here

Owning a dog seems to result in buying all sorts of "essential" paraphernalia. To keep it all neat and tidy in one place, why not make this handy little wall shelf reserved for all things dog? Treats can sit up on top in the fancy containers you have made, while leads, dog towels, and your Hanging Toy Basket (see page 70) can all be hung underneath.

handy wall shelf

(see page 70)

YOU WILL NEED

2 pieces of wood approx. 12 × 3½ × ¾ inches (30 × 9 × 2cm) (an ideal project to reuse odd bits of wood)

wood glue

3–4 1¼-inch (3cm) wood screws

screwdriver

medium-grain sandpaper

paint in your color of choice—small sample pots are ideal for this but will need waxing afterwards to keep them in good condition

paintbrush

2 small screw-eye hooks*

2 screw-in door knobs

1 cup hook

1 Assemble your shelf by gluing along the long ¾-inch (2cm) thick edge and placing one piece of wood on top of the other in an L-shape, then screw them together at the seam. This will ensure you have a firm and sturdy shelf. Leave to dry for at least 24 hours.

2 Sand any rough edges and apply your first coat of paint. Let dry. Repeat until you are happy with the finish. Apply wax if needed.

3 On the top edge of the shelf, mark in 2 inches (5cm) from each edge and screw in your eyelet hooks as close to the back edge of the wood as possible.

4 Mark on the shelf front where you want to place your knobs and cup hook and screw them in.

5 Fix your shelf to the wall by screwing through the screw-eye hooks, then place all your doggie gear in its new home.

You may wish to use a method of attachment more suitable for your wall.

Every dog needs a name banner to hang up high and proclaim "this is my stuff." Hang this carefully stitched banner above your dog's bed, over the Handy Wall Shelf (see page 42), or in a special corner that gets the most sun and a carefully positioned cushion can be found.

"*this is me*" name banner

(see page 42)

YOU WILL NEED

various pieces of mismatched fabric

lace and ribbon trimmings

needle and black embroidery floss

ribbon

1 Cut a piece of fabric to the size you would like your banner (this one is 9 × 6 inches [22 × 15cm]) and neaten the edges with an overlock or zigzag stitch.

2 Pin the lace and trimmings onto the fabric until you are happy with the layout, and then stitch them down by hand.

3 Mark out your dog's name onto the banner and then backstitch the name onto the fabric using the embroidery floss.

4 Stitch two pieces of ribbon to each of the top corners and hang your banner for all to see.

Take a little piece of home with you to give your dog comfort when you are traveling far and wide. This roll-up bed is easy to keep in the trunk of the car and will provide your dog with the perfect place to sleep when you are out and about exploring the countryside, staying with friends or on vacation.

traveling dog bed

YOU WILL NEED

a 2 × 40-inch (5 ×100cm) strip of waxed cotton

25½ × 37½-inch (65 × 95cm) piece of waxed cotton for bed bottom

25½ × 37½-inch (65 × 95cm) piece fabric of your choice for bed top

24¼ × 36¼-inch (62 × 92cm) piece of cotton batting

tailor's chalk

a long darning needle and strong linen thread

1 Make the traveling bed tie by folding the strip of waxed cotton in half, right sides together, and stitching down the length of the strip leaving a ½-inch (1cm) seam. Trim the seam allowance and turn the piece to the right side.

2 Fold the raw bottom edges of the tie to the inside and press. Top-stitch around all sides making sure you stitch the two ends closed. Fold the tie in half lengthwise.

3 Mark the center point of the waxed cotton for the bed bottom along the short edge on the wrong side and then lay the fold of the fabric tie in line with the edge of the fabric piece, strips facing toward the middle of the fabric. Baste stitch in place.

4 Pin the bed top and bottom pieces right sides together, making sure your tie is sandwiched in between the two, and stitch a ½-inch (1cm) seam around the edges, leaving a 12-inch (30cm) gap at the end opposite the ties.

5 Snip the excess fabric at the corners, trim the seam allowances, and then turn the bed to the right side, easing out the corners.

6 Place the piece of batting inside the cover and smooth it out so that it lays flat inside, the corners are in corners, and there are no lumps or bumps. Stitch the opening closed.

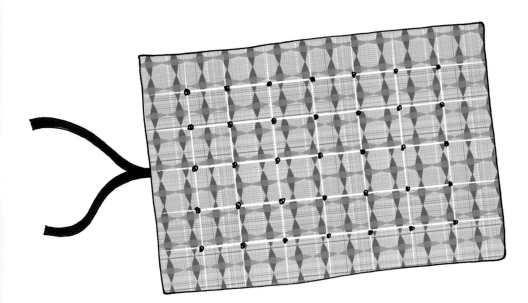

7 Using tailor's chalk, measure out seven lines spaced 3 inches (8cm) apart across the bed top. Repeat with five lines spaced 4¾ inches (12cm) apart down the length of the bed to create a grid.

8 Using a strong thread and long needle, pass the needle through the point where the lines cross (see above). Bring the needle back through and tie the thread in a tight knot. Snip the thread. Repeat this until you have a grid of knots securing all the layers of the fabric, making a quilt-like effect.

9 Roll up the bed and secure it with ties until your dog needs to rest its weary head.

Everyone deserves a treat at Christmas, including the critters in your home. Make this paw-shaped Christmas stocking and fill it with all kinds of handmade goodness, including toys, a fancy new collar, and delicious things to munch and chew.

Christmas stocking

YOU WILL NEED

20 × 20-inch (50 × 50cm) piece fake fur fabric

15¾ × 15¾-inch (40 × 40cm) piece felt or wool

15¾ × 15¾-inch (40 × 40cm) piece fusible web interfacing (such as Wonder Under)

a strip of contrast fabric—twice the width of the top of the stocking + ¾ × 5½ inches (2 × 14cm)

a small piece of ribbon to use as a hanger

1 Enlarge the stocking and paw templates on page 52 by 200% and use as a pattern to cut out the fabric. Pin the stocking template to the wrong side of the fake fur fabric and cut out the shape. Repeat for the other side.

2 Trace your paw shape onto the paper side of the interfacing, then iron onto the wrong side of your felt or wool square. Cut out the paw shape and remove the backing paper. Using a warm iron and a cloth, press them to the right side of one of the stocking pieces.

3 Stitch around the edge of the paw shapes. You can use either a narrow zigzag stitch or free-hand embroidery, depending on what you prefer.

4 Lay the two stocking pieces down, right sides facing, and pin around the edge. You may wish to tack the edge before you stitch to keep both pieces perfectly aligned. Stitch around the edge, then zigzag or overlock the seam to prevent it from fraying. Turn out to the right side.

5 Pin the hanging ribbon to the top edge of the stocking on the wrong side, near the side seam with the loop side facing downward.

6 Fold the strip of contrast fabric in half and stitch the short side with a ½-inch (1 cm) seam to create a band of fabric. Fold it in half lengthwise with the wrong sides facing and press along the entire length to create a sharp fold.

7 Pin the band around the top of the stocking, with the right side of the band facing the wrong side of the stocking. Stitch together using a ½-inch (1 cm) seam, ensuring you stitch the hanging loop between the band and stocking. Fold the band to the right side of the stocking and press.

To have better control of the fur fabric it is easier to cut each piece separately rather than together.

Christmas stocking
enlarge template 200%

play

When your dog isn't sleeping, eating, or barking at something outside, they are playing. Make them a basket full of toys to throw and catch until they are ready to collapse in the corner with a heart full of joy.

Your dog will love chasing after this ball stuffed full of fabric scraps. Its practical handle helps you to chuck it just a little bit farther, which may wear your dog out a little bit quicker. It can also be thrown in the washing machine if it gets too dirty ... hours of fun for you both.

chuck-it fabric ball

YOU WILL NEED

8 × 20-inch (20 × 50cm) piece of fabric or six 8 × 3-inch (20 × 8cm) pieces if you would like to use different fabrics

2 pieces of cotton twill tape 18 inches (45cm) long

small fabric scraps for stuffing

strong thread and needle

1 Enlarge the ball template on page 58 by 120%, and use it as a pattern to cut out 6 pieces of fabric.

2 With right sides facing, pin and stitch 3 pieces of fabric together and then repeat with the other 3 pieces.

3 Place a piece of twill tape onto the opposite edges of one of the three stitched sections of the ball at the notch mark, making sure the tape is lying on the right side of the fabric toward the center of the ball. Stitch into place, sewing back and forth several times to attach the handle firmly.

4 With right sides facing and the twill tape inside the ball, sew the two remaining sides of the ball together, leaving an opening in one side to insert the stuffing.

5 Fill the ball with small scraps of fabric and then stitch the opening closed with strong thread.

6 Hand stitch across each seam from the top to the bottom of outside of the ball to give it extra strength.

7 Tie knots in your twill tape to form a handle with which to throw the ball.

You can leave out the handle if you prefer. If you would like to make a different size, just enlarge or reduce the pattern on a photocopier until you achieve your desired size of ball.

chuck-it fabric ball

enlarge template 120%

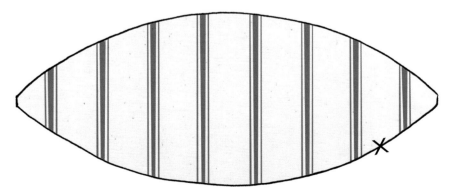

This toy was inspired by a rather wayward Jack Russell who liked to raid the recycling basket and spend his days dashing about the place with a plastic bottle in tow, making a rather gleeful *grrrrr* sound. To make a toy that will last just a little bit longer, I added a cover that could be reused once the bottle inside had died a horrible chewed-up death. It also has the added bonus of preventing the plastic inside the cover from being swallowed by your dog.

It has been designed for a regular pint plastic water bottle—you may need to tinker with the measurements to fit your usual brand.

grrrr toy

YOU WILL NEED

an empty plastic bottle (about 16 ounces/1 pint)

10 × 10-inch (25 × 25cm) piece non-fraying fabric for top of cover, such as fleece, felt, or a piece of wool blanket

10 × 10-inch (25 × 25cm) piece sturdy fabric for bottom of cover (recycled jeans are excellent for this)

6¼-inch (16cm) piece of ½-inch (1cm) wide elastic

1 Neaten the edges of the bottom piece of your cover fabric with either an overlock or narrow zigzag stitch.

2 Lay the two pieces of top and bottom fabric together with right sides facing and stitch a ½-inch (1cm) seam allowance along one side.

3 Lay the cover flat and cut the top fleece part of the cover into strips leaving about ¾ inch (2cm) uncut at the base (see diagram above). Knot the top of each strip.

4 Fold your cover lengthwise with right sides facing, and stitch the side seam of the bottom denim piece only. Leave the fleece seam open.

5 At the base, turn under a ⅔-inch (15mm) hem to create a channel for the elastic. Stitch the seam, leaving an opening to thread the elastic through. Thread the elastic through the opening and stitch the ends firmly together and then stitch the opening shut.

6 Sew a line of gathering stitches along the top of the uncut fleece just below the strips. Place your bottle inside the cover and then gather the fleece together tightly and stitch through several times to secure the top of the cover. The bottle can be easily removed and replaced through the elastic opening at the base.

Don't forget to remove the bottle top and ring before inserting the bottle into the cover as they may be a choking hazard.

If you want to add any embroidery or decoration to the lower part of the cover, do this before you begin to assemble the pieces.

Does your dog like to catch their toys in mid-air, leaping from the ground to make that amazing save? If yes, then one or two of these frisbees are essential in your dog's toy box.

fetch frisbee

1 Measure thirty 72-inch (2m) lengths of yarn. A quick and easy way to do this is to wind the yarn around a yard piece of wood or ruler and cut through the yarn at one end.

2 Lay the yarn lengths together and secure one end by winding a strong thread several times around the yarn and sewing a couple of stitches to secure it.

3 Separate the yarn into 3 groups of 10 strands each and then tightly braid them together until you have reached the end. Secure as before, by winding strong thread around them. Don't break the thread.

4 Wrap the braid into a spiral around the end with the unbroken thread, stitching it together tightly as you go. Continue to wrap and stitch until you reach the end of the braid. Use several stitches to make sure the end is fastened in place.

5 Trim any excess yarn at both ends of your frisbee and gently squeeze a couple of drops of Superglue onto the thread to seal it and stop it from fraying.

 You can replace the yarn with polar fleece, T-shirt yarn, denim, or strong cotton if you wish.

Dogs always need another toy and this toy is a great fabric stash buster—it's a handy size and weight for a game of fetch, or catch, run off, and chew, depending on how your dog likes to play.

throw-and-catch bone

YOU WILL NEED

2 pieces of fabric large enough to fit your template

polyester cushion filling

strong needle and thread

1 Using the bone template on page 41, cut out two bone shapes from your fabric and then pin them together, right sides facing.

2 Using a short stitch, sew around the edge of the bone leaving the seam open where indicated on the template. Turn the fabric open and sew the seam again following the previous line of stitches. This will make sure you have a really strong seam.

3 Trim the seam allowance and snip the seams on all the curves.

4 Turn the bone to the right side and stuff with polyester filling until really firm. Hand stitch the opening closed.

These jute strips are really quick and easy to crochet and will give your dog something to chew and throw about, plus with the jute string working like dental floss, they will help keep teeth and gums healthy.

chew-it strips

YOU WILL NEED

ball of jute string
H/8 crochet hook

1 Chain 6 for your foundation row. Turn.

2 In the third chain from the hook, work a half double crochet, then work 1 half double crochet in each of the next 4 stitches. Turn.

3 Chain 2 and then 1 half double crochet in each stitch until the end. Turn.

4 Repeat step 3 until you have 16 rows.

5 Bind off the last stitch and sew in the excess threads at each end so that they are unlikely to come undone when your dog is playing with the strips.

hanging toy basket

Dogs have a tendency to leave their toys all over the house, especially in places where you are most likely to step on them. Keep them all together safely out of the way with this nifty hanging basket, hung from a hook or door handle. Both you and your dog will know where their favorite squeaker is at all times.

YOU WILL NEED

120-yard (130m) ball jute twine (such as Nutscene garden twine)
I/9 crochet hook

1 Chain 5 and join the ring with a slip stitch into the first stitch.

2 Work 8 single crochet into the middle of the ring. Join with a slip stitch into the first stitch.

3 Chain 2, work 1 half double crochet in same stitch. Then 2 half double crochet into each of the next 7 stitches. Join with a slip stich into the second chain stitch. (16 stitches)

4 Chain 2, work *1 half double crochet into next stitch, 2 half double crochet into following stitch. Repeat from * to the end. Join with a slip stitch into the second chain stitch. (24 stitches)

5 Chain 2, work *1 half double crochet into each of the next 2 stitches, then 2 half double crochet into following stitch. Repeat from * to end. Join with a slip stitch into the second chain stitch. (32 stitches)

6 Chain 2, work *1 half double crochet into each of next 3 stitches, then 2 half double crochet into the following stitch. Repeat from *to end. Join with a slip stitch into the second chain stitch. (40 stitches)

7 Chain 2, work *1 half double crochet into next 4 stitches, then 2 half double crochet into the following stitch. Repeat from * to end. Join with a slip stitch into the second chain stitch. (48 stitches)

8 Chain 2, work 1 half double crochet into each stitch to end. Join with a slip stitch into the second chain stitch. Repeat step 8 for 10 more rows.

9 Chain 1, work single crochet into each stitch to end. Join with a slip stitch into the first chain.

10 Work a slip stitch into each of the next 3 single crochet and then chain 20. Count back 6 single crochet and attach the chain into the 6th single crochet space with a slip stitch.

11 Work 20 single crochet along the chain to form a hanging loop. Slip stitch into the last chain. Sew in the ends so the loop is secure.

Most dogs like nothing more than a mindless game of throw and fetch. Jute string is a cheap and natural material that makes a strong toy for your dog to enjoy but also has the benefit of cleaning your dog's teeth when they bite into it.

braided fetch toy

YOU WILL NEED

I ball of jute string, cut into thirty 18-inch (45cm) lengths

1 Lay the lengths of jute together, then tie one end into a firm knot, making sure there are no loose strands.

2 Separate the strings into 3 groups of 10 strands each.

3 Start to braid the string, taking care to keep it tight as you work. Once you have braided approximately two-thirds of the length, tie a tight knot at the bottom end. Again, make sure all the strings are pulled tightly into the knot.

4 Throw your toy and then hope that your dog brings it back…

If you wish, you can make a much longer braid. When you have completed the steps above, tie another knot in the middle of the toy to give your dog something to grab onto.

wear

A coat of fur is all a dog really needs, but a fancy collar, jaunty neck scarf, or a stylish coat to keep out the chill wind are a few of the projects you can make to keep your dog looking their best each and every day.

bow tie for boys

Does your dog have a dapper way about him,
a gentlemanly air as he chews his bone? If so, a
bow tie sounds right up his alley. Add a collar
cover (see page 100) and turn your pooch into
quite the gentleman as you stroll him around the
neighborhood.

1 With the right sides facing, pin the two 5½ × 4-inch (14 × 10cm) pieces of fabric together, then stitch a ½-inch (1cm) seam allowance around the edge, leaving a small opening.

2 Trim the excess fabric from the corners and turn your rectangle of fabric right side out. Gently ease out the corners and seams and press into shape with an iron, then top stitch around the edge to close the opening.

3 Neaten the two long edges of the fabric strip by stitching a ¼-inch (5mm) wide hem on each side. Neaten the short ends with an over lock or zigzag stitch to keep them from fraying.

4 Wrap your strip around the middle of the rectangle to create a bow-tie shape and hand stitch the ends in place.

5 Join the ends of each piece of elastic together to form two loops, then stitch them both onto the back of the bow tie.

6 Slip onto your dog's collar at a jaunty angle for the world to see what a gentleman he truly is.

Ladies like to adorn themselves with pretty things, so why not make this sweet felt flower to give your pooch a bit of flair to wear on dull days? Choose bright, eye-catching colors and match with a Nifty Dog-Collar Cover (see page 100) for a pooch who turns heads as she meanders along the street.

fancy flower for girls

YOU WILL NEED

2 sheets of different-colored felt (approx. 12 × 12 inches [30 × 30cm])

needle and thread to match the felt

2 inches (5cm) of 1-inch (2.5cm) wide elastic

1 Cut a 1¼ × 12-inch (3 × 30cm) strip from each sheet of felt.

2 Cut scallops along the edge of one piece and then cut notches along the second strip (see diagrams on page 80).

3 With the thread doubled, sew gathering stitches along the straight edge of the scalloped piece of felt and tightly gather it into a flower shape, securing it with several small stitches.

4 To make the center of the flower, make several cuts along the length of the notched strip, ensuring you don't cut all the way through, then roll it up. Secure the bundle with a few small stitches and then sew it to the middle of the felt flower. Don't skimp on the stitches, as it needs to be attached firmly.

5 Cut a small circle from the remaining felt and firmly stitch this to the back of the flower to hold everything in place.

6 Fold the elastic in half, stitch the two ends together so it forms a loop, and sew it onto the back of the flower.

7 The flower is now ready to slide onto your dog's collar.

*No day is
complete
without
wearing your
favorite
felt flowers…*

fancy flower for girls

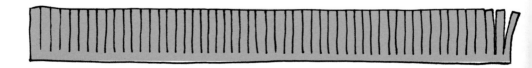

There's nothing more pleasing than seeing a dog sporting a dashing neckerchief, but they do have a tendency to cast them aside in the long grass while they are hunting for various small animals. To solve this problem, make your dog a handsome neckerchief that attaches to their collar—there will be no more glum faces or doggy sad eyes at a favorite scarf lost forever in the undergrowth.

jaunty neckerchief

YOU WILL NEED

2 squares of 9 × 9-inch (22 × 22cm) contrasting fabric

1 With the right sides facing, pin the fabric and stitch a ½-inch (1cm) seam around the edge, stitching across two of the corners (as shown below), leaving an opening to turn the fabric inside out.

2 Trim the corners of any excess fabric, then turn your fabric right side out and gently ease out the corners and seams.

3 Press into shape with an iron, taking care that the seam at the opening is tucked inside. Pin to keep it in place.

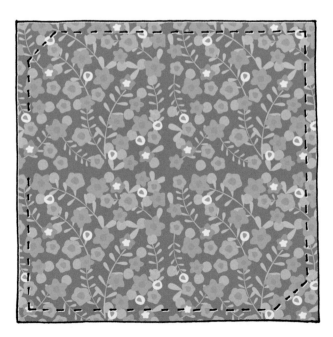

4 Top stitch about ⅛ inch (3mm) from the edge around the entire piece; this will neatly close the open seam.

5 Fold the square in half diagonally, corner to furthest corner, and press.

6 Lay your dog's collar along the fold and mark the stitch line. Remember to allow a little extra for the depth of the collar (about ⅛–¼ inch [3–5mm]).

7 Stitch along this line to create a channel to hold the collar.

8 Thread the collar through the channel and pop onto your dog.

This scarf fits a medium-sized dog. If you wish to make the scarf bigger or smaller, depending on the size of your dog, just adjust the size of the squares as you desire.

Even the most robust of dogs feel the chill of a cold and blustery day. They may give you those "let's stay by the fire" eyes as you grab your coat and their lead. Why not give them a little extra warmth and keep the wind at bay by crocheting this rather lovely cowl? Team it with the Dandy Dog Coat on page 92 and your pooch will be ready to walk in all weather.

keep-warm crochet cowl

YOU WILL NEED

Worsted-weight yarn in 2 colors
I/9 crochet hook

Main Cowl

1 Measure around the widest part of your dog's neck and add ¾ inch (2cm) (measurement A).

2 Measure from the base of the neck at the shoulders to just below the ears (measurement B).

3 Work a multiple of 3 chain for your foundation row until it reaches measurement A.

4 Slip stitch into the first chain to create a ring.

5 Chain 3 (counts as the first double), then work 2 double crochet into the same stitch.

6 Skip 2 stitches.

7 Work 3 double crochet in the next chain stitch and repeat to the end of the row.

8 Slip stitch into the third chain.

9 Chain 3 (the first double), then in each group of 3 doubles, work *1 treble in space between #1 and #2 doubles, 1 chain, 1 double in the space between doubles #2 and #3. Repeat from * to the last group of 3 double crochet, then work 1 double, 1 chain and slip stitch into the third chain.

10 Chain 3, 3 double crochet into each 1 chain space until the last space, then work 2 doubles and slip stitch into the third chain.

11 Work steps 9 and 10 until the cowl reaches measurement B, then sew in the ends.

Top edge

1 Join the yarn into any space on the bottom edge. Work 1 single crochet into each stitch until the end, then slip stitch into the first single crochet.

2 Chain 1, then single crochet into each stitch. Slip stitch into the first single crochet.

3 Work *1 slip stitch into each of the next 2 stitches, slip stitch, chain 3, slip stitch into the next stitch, making a picot, then repeat from * to the end and sew in the ends.

Bottom edge

1 Join the yarn into any space on the top edge. Work 1 single crochet into each stitch until the end.

2 Slip stitch into the first single crochet and sew in the ends.

As every dog owner knows, bathing a dog can be a rather soggy experience. Trying to negotiate wrapping them in a towel while lifting them from the bath often leads to disaster, and the dog's determination to get away and have a good shake is second to none. By adapting a bath sheet this task becomes a breeze and a dry bathroom is an added bonus.

bath-day towel

YOU WILL NEED

1 large bath sheet (40 × 60 inch [100 × 150cm])

7 yards (6m) bias binding

scraps of contrast fabric or felt for a paw-print motif, optional

1 Begin by cutting a 40-inch (100cm) square from the towel. Save the excess piece to use later.

2 Lay the towel out flat. Starting from one corner measure and mark 8 inches (20cm) down. Repeat on the opposite side. Draw a line across and cut along it to remove the corner piece of fabric. Place to one side.

3 Cut a 20-inch (50cm) square from the excess fabric, then cut it in half to make two triangles.

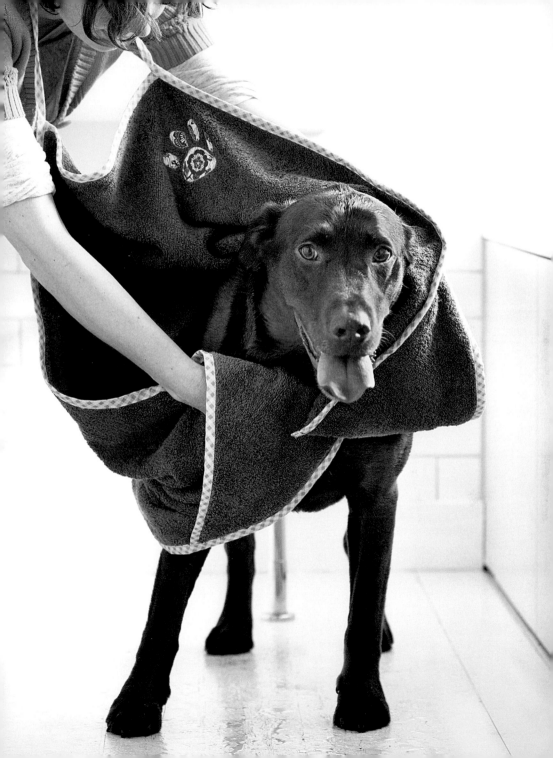

4 Stitch bias binding across the diagonal to seal the raw edge.

5 With the flat part of the main towel at the top, pin the two triangle pieces to opposite corners with the bias binding facing the middle to form pockets.

6 Tack the outside seams of the pockets (the pockets are for you, not the dog!) as this will make stitching easier when you are adding the bias tape.

7 Stitch bias binding around the entire edge of the towel, making sure you secure all layers at the pocket corners.

8 To make the neck strap (which goes over your head, not the dog's!) cut a 20-inch (50cm) piece of bias binding and fold it in half, then stitch together along the long side. Fold over each end into the inside to neaten.

9 Attach one end of your strap to the towel and stitch on. Before you stitch the other side, pin the strap and try it on around your head, making adjustments to the length if necessary.

10 To add a paw print motif, cut out the shape from some contrasting fabric and then pin onto your towel. Using a narrow zigzag stitch on your sewing machine, stitch around the outside edges to secure your shape to the towel. Immediately give your dog a bath to give your towel a whirl.

There are days when your dog needs a little help keeping cozy and snug when venturing out of the house. This toasty overcoat will keep your pooch warm and dry on the windiest and wettest of days, with the added bonus of helping to minimize the amount of mess and debris that your dog will collect in their coat and sneak back into the house. Team it with the crochet cowl (see page 85) and your dog will be prepared whatever the weather.

dandy dog coat

YOU WILL NEED

paper for template

20 inches (50cm) waxed cotton or similar waterproof fabric (you may need more if you have a large dog)

20 inches (50cm) polar fleece fabric

6 inches (15mm) sew-on Velcro, or a hook and loop fastener

Before you begin, you will need to take the following measurements from your dog. Have a few treats on hand to get them to stand still.

A measure from the base of the neck (just below collar) to the tail, then add ¾ inch (2cm).

B measure around the rib cage behind the front legs. Halve this measurement, then add 2 inches (5cm).

C measure around the front of the chest from behind the front legs. Halve this measurement, then add ¾ inches (2cm).

D measure around the neck just below where the collar sits, then divide by three.

1 Once you have all your dog's measurements, make a paper template, starting by drawing a rectangle using measurements A and B on a large folded piece of paper.

2 At the bottom right hand corner, extend the line by measurement C, then draw a line up 4 inches (10cm) (see i on page 94).

3 Divide measurement D in half and mark this point from the top-right corner (see ii on page 94).

4 Join points (i) and (ii) with a gentle curve, then round off the bottom left

corner and the front strap corners. Cut a 3 × 10-inch (8 × 25cm) paper belly strap.

5 Try the paper pattern on your dog; attach the belly strap just behind the front legs, then adjust the length for a comfy fit.

6 When you are happy with the fit, cut two of each of your patterns (including the belly strap) per fabric: one set from the waterproof fabric and one set from the polar fleece.

7 With the right sides facing, pin your fabric. If you are using waxed cotton, pin in the seam allowance and remove the pins as you sew so you don't damage the fabric.

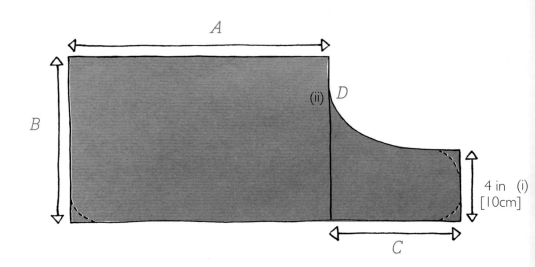

8 Stitch around the edge, leaving an opening on the back edge to allow you to turn the coat.

9 Trim the fabric at the curves and turn it right side out, carefully easing out the seams. Press gently using an iron. If the fabric is waxed cotton, use a piece of greaseproof paper to protect your iron.

10 Sew two lines of top stitch, the first close to the edge to close the opening, and then another about ¼ inch (5mm) in from the first.

11 Cut 4 inches (10cm) of Velcro and stitch it onto the chest straps.

12 Repeat steps 7–10 for the belly strap.

13 Pin the belly strap to one side of the coat and stitch using a double line of stitches to make sure it stays put.

14 On the opposite end of the belly strap, stitch one side of your Velcro. Try the coat on your dog and mark where to stitch the other piece of Velcro, making sure that it is a snug fit but not so tight that it restricts movement. Then, stitch the second piece of Velcro onto the coat.

The paper template can be used to try the coat out for size on your dog and make adjustments before you cut your fabric. Remember, the template allows for seams so it will be a little bigger than the finished coat.

A wonderful long walk with your dog is often blighted by the subsequent muddy-paw mess that follows at home. This towel is quick and easy to use on muddy paws and should cut down on the mess unleashed on your floors.

muddy-paw towel

YOU WILL NEED

1 bath towel
3 yards (3m) of ¾-inch (2cm) wide bias binding tape
small piece of ribbon
small fabric pieces for paw print, optional

1 Begin by cutting a 10 × 43-inch (25 × 110cm) rectangle from the bath towel (adjust length if your towel comes up shorter).

2 Cut two 10 × 12-inch (25 × 30cm) pocket pieces from the remaining bath towel and place to one side.

3 Fold the rectangle in half lengthwise and mark and round off the corners. You may want to create a paper template for the rounded corners to make sure both sides are equal.

4 On one short edge of a pocket piece, bind the raw edge with bias tape. Repeat for the second piece. If you are adding a paw print design, stitch it onto the pocket now (instructions are as for bath towel; see page 88).

5 Pin the pocket pieces to each end of the rectangle and round off the corners to match. Tack them down, as this will make it easier when adding the bias tape.

6 Sew bias binding tape around the edges, ensuring that both layers are covered at the pocket ends.

7 Sew the ribbon about halfway along the rectangle so you can hang the towel up in easy reach of the door.

8 To use the towel, place your hands into the pockets and rub your dog's paws to remove the mud—and save yourself a whole lot of floor-mopping.

crochet handle
for dull dog leads

Dog leads are not the most attractive things for your dog to wear. They are practical, they keep your dog safe in sticky situations that he or she may stumble into on your daily walk, but— let's face it—they are dull. This colorful handle cover brightens up the dullest of dog leads and makes it a little more comfortable for your hands when faced with unruly pulling.

YOU WILL NEED

sport weight yarn in various colors
F/5 crochet hook
yarn needle

1 Chain 10 for your foundation row (check that this will fit around your lead handle and add or subtract stitches accordingly). Turn.

2 Chain 2 , then 1 single crochet into each stitch. Turn and repeat for the following rows.

3 Work as many rows in each color as you like and keep checking the length around the handle as you work. When changing to a new shade, sew in the ends, leaving one long piece of yarn. You will use this to join the handle around the lead.

4 When you have reached your desired length, cast off, then wrap the cover around the handle of your lead, joining the long edges facing the middle.

5 Carefully stitch the edges together using the yarn tails left from each color, then sew in the ends and take your dog out for a walk.

Dog collars can be tricky things to keep clean and, as they are worn all the time, they have a tendency to smell a bit. These collar covers add a jazzy, lively print or two to your dog's wardrobe, and they can be removed and popped into the washing machine to keep your pooch's collar smelling A-Okay.

nifty dog-collar covers

YOU WILL NEED

paper for template
strip of fabric 2.5
times wider than your
dog's collar

1 Measure from the D-ring to the hole that you use to fasten the collar and add ¾ inches (2cm).

2 Measure the width of the collar, double it, then add ½ inch (1cm).

3 Make a paper template using the collar measurements, pin it to the fabric, and cut out the pattern.

4 Turn over a ½-inch (1cm) seam on either end with the wrong sides facing. Press it with an iron and stitch along ¼ inch (5mm) from the edge.

5 With the right sides facing, fold the piece of fabric in half and pin it in place. Stitch a ½-inch (1cm) seam along the length of the fabric. Overlock or trim ¼ inch (5mm) from the seam allowance, then use a narrow zigzag stitch to finish the seam.

6 Turn out the collar cover to the right side using a loop turner or good old safety pin and slip onto the collar, then gently iron the seam open, taking care with the heat setting, especially if your dog's collar is made of leather.

Treat your dog to a shiny new collar and use it to make a template for the cover before they start wearing it and making it smelly.

resources

Don't just limit yourself to pet shops when buying bits and pieces for your dog. Keep an eye out in thrift stores as many of them have a special "dog" blanket and towel box in which many a treasure can be found. Always be on the look-out for old woolen clothing, enamel bowls, and tins as you can never have enough when it comes to pets of a doggy nature.

eat

Cutters
If a bone-shaped cookie cutter takes your fancy and you can't find one anywhere, try
www.bedbathandbeyond.com or
www.walmart.com

Plastic dog food lids
www.petsathome.com

play

Jute string
Nutscene's jute string is the only string that I have been able to use to crochet, plus they have the most fab colors.
www.nutscene.com or
www.amazon.com

Fusible web interfacing (Wonder Under)
www.amazon.com

nest

Aran yarn
Woolcraft, Sirdar, and James C Brett all do excellent yarns that will wash and wash no matter how much your dog tries to scruff them up. Also try your local independent wool shop or search for online stockists.
www.us.deramores.com
www.michaels.com
www.loveknitting.com
www.craftsy.com
www.yarn.com

Dog-friendly fabrics
Most of the fabric used in this book can be found at your local fabric shop. Or look online if you have trouble finding fur and fleece fabric.
www.fabric.com

wear

Waxed fabric
This is pretty much impossible to find, except on good old eBay.
www.ebay.com

index

acknowledgments

This book is dedicated to all the dogs that have crossed my path over the years, but especially Paddy the Poodle, who patiently allowed my sister and I to dress him up for hours on end in various ridiculous outfits. To Stanley, who has been measured, modeled, and made to sit for ages while I road tested the patterns and rudely removed from cushions and blankets when he tried to sneak in a quick nap.

To Judith, for coming up with this crazy idea of writing the book; it has been such fun and I'm sorry for laughing at you when you suggested it. To Claire, for sorting out all the bits and bobs and everyone else at Kyle Books who beaver on behind the scenes making books happen.

To Mark, for the great design, and especially to Dudley, Casper, and Miss Mollie, who stole a little bit of my heart forever.

To Kate and Polly and your doggy pals for fab photos and styling. I am more than a little bit chuffed.

A big thank you to Mungo and Maud, Purple Bone, Holly and Lil, and Verve-London for lending us all sorts of doggy paraphernalia to get the great shots throughout the book.

And last but not least to all you dog owners out there who are feeling a little crafty. Making something for your dog might not be the quickest and easiest path, considering that there is every possibility that it may be destroyed in 10 seconds flat, but you will enjoy every step of the process and your heart will shine when you see them snuggled up on the bed you made or proudly strutting their fancy collar in the park.

the models

Dudley

Zippy

Peggy

Digby

Miss Mollie

Badger

Raj

Stanley

Bella

Sweep

Chocky

Casper

Moses

Editor, STC edition: Cristina Garces
Cover Design, STC edition: Deb Wood
Production Manager, STC edition: Jake Wilburn
Project Editor: Judith Hannam
Designer: Mark Latter

Library of Congress Control Number: 2015948558

ISBN: 978-1-61769-192-8

Printed and bound in China
10 9 8 7 6 5 4 3 2 1

Stewart, Tabori & Chang products are available at special discounts when purchased
in quantity for premiums and promotions as well as fundraising or educational use.
Special editions can also be created to specification. For details, contact specialsales@
abramsbooks.com or the address below.

ABRAMS
THE ART OF BOOKS SINCE 1949
115 West 18th Street
New York, NY 10011
www.abramsbooks.com

A house is cold and empty without a four-legged friend